Waltzing through
the Endtime

DAVID BOTTOMS

Waltzing through the Endtime

COPPER CANYON PRESS

BOOKS BY DAVID BOTTOMS

POETRY

Waltzing through the Endtime
Oglethorpe's Dream
Vagrant Grace
Armored Hearts: Selected and New Poems
Under the Vulture-Tree
In a U-Haul North of Damascus
Shooting Rats at the Bibb County Dump
Jamming with the Band at the VFW

NOVELS

Easter Weekend
Any Cold Jordan

ANTHOLOGY

The Morrow Anthology of Younger American Poets
(editor)

Printed in the United States of America

Cover art: Purvis Young, *Cross & Angel Over City*, ca 1991, paint on wood, 49½ x 32½ inches. Courtesy of Skot Foreman Fine Art.

Copper Canyon Press is in residence under the auspices of the Centrum Foundation at Fort Worden State Park in Port Townsend, Washington. Centrum sponsors artist residencies, education workshops for Washington State students and teachers, Blues, Jazz, and Fiddle Tunes festivals, classical music performances, and the Port Townsend Writers' Conference.

LIBRARY OF CONGRESS CATALOGING-IN-PUBLICATION DATA
Bottoms, David.
  Waltzing through the endtime / David Bottoms.
      p. cm.
  ISBN 1-55659-215-9 (pbk. : alk. paper)
  I. Title.
  PS3552.O819w35 2004
  811'.54—dc22

                           2004010107

COPPER CANYON PRESS
Post Office Box 271
Port Townsend, Washington 98368
www.coppercanyonpress.org

ACKNOWLEDGMENTS

Grateful acknowledgment is made to the editors of the following publications, in which these poems first appeared: "Three-quarter Moon and Moment of Grace" (in a different version) in *The Atlanta Journal-Constitution*; "Black Hawk Rag," "Disobedience," "Kenny Roebuck's Knuckle-Curve," "Shooting Rats in the Afterlife" in *The Georgia Review*; "Homage to Buck Cline," "Little Drop of Wickedness" in *The Kenyon Review*; "Vigilance" in *The Oxford American*; "Andalusia Visit" in *The Paris Review*; "Easter Shoes Epistle," "O Mandolin, *O Magnum Mysterium*," "Melville in the Bass Boat," "The Undertaker" in *Poetry*; "Allatoona Storm" in *Sewanee Theological Review*; "In the Big House of the Allman Brothers My Heart Gets Tuned" in *The Southern Review*.

"Andalusia Visit" also appeared in *Flannery O'Connor: In Celebration of Genius*, edited by Sarah Gordon, Hill Street Press.

"O Mandolin, *O Magnum Mysterium*" was awarded the 2002 Frederick Bock Prize from *Poetry*. Sincere thanks to the editors of *Poetry* and to the donors of the prize.

The author also gratefully acknowledges the generous support of the John Simon Guggenheim Memorial Foundation.

for Kelly and Rachel

Darest thou now O soul,
Walk out with me toward the unknown region,
Where neither ground is for the feet nor any path to follow?

WALT WHITMAN

... the greatest dramas naturally involve the salvation
or loss of the soul.

FLANNERY O'CONNOR

CONTENTS

I

Easter Shoes Epistle

for Mark Jarman

Yesterday morning five plumbers from Sundance
dug up the pipes in our front yard —

                          twelve feet down and roots
through a joint, a total blockage.
Now mounds of sour mud sag beside a canvas tarp, while the last rain
      dripping
like wax through the Bradford pears, glistens
on the boxwoods.
                Stench and flowers, and an urgent glaze
over the neighborhood, the dogwoods already mustering an incredible
      witness,
and the jungles of hydrangea,
                     the Japanese cherries, the azaleas deviling
the roses, and oddly, in the street,
even an old work boot, like a shriveled potato,
rain-curled, corroded,
           shooting its little feelers toward the curb.

Every leaf an oracle, sure,
              and in the local phone book
not one listing under *mystagogue*...

———

Every spring
the world is such a tricky magician, tugging whole maple trees
out of its black silk hat, pulling thunderstorms
from its sleeve...

Miracle or sleight of hand
is what I fret about.
                        And the mockingbird, unconcerned, goes on worrying
the new weeds, and the cardinal,
the chipmunk homesteading the overturned wheelbarrow,
our neighbor's grouchy tabby
                        skulking about in its own eternal moment.

Only we have to travel on faith,
                        struggling not to notice the absence,
the stray shoe in the street, the fugitive foot...

—————

Saturday night, just after supper, aftertaste of vegetable soup
and soda crackers
washed down with chocolate milk...

A little blue moonlight spilling across the sink,
the pans of sudsy water,
                        the Easter petunia sagging in its grim plastic pot,
a little moonlight, I remember, slipping past the ragged pines
screening out the lights
on the radio tower... blue flash, blue flash...

Just like an old shoe, my mother said, rattling her bottle of polish,
meaning *faith*,
                        while I glanced at my loafers on the seat of a kitchen chair —
penny loafers, sans pennies, scuffed around the toes and cracking,
run-down in schoolyards, filth of pasture,
                        polluted creek.

—————

Sometimes faith is more a stale cracker,
                        and yet how little else

we have to share — a few words, a few dried metaphors we can lay aboard,
stocking up like Noah for that darkest flood.

Little cakes and wine,
Lawrence advised, a few cooking pots, a change of clothes.
And a good pair of shoes, I'd say,
                              a can of Kiwi, a bottle of Griffin.

                              ____

Or plain old saddle soap will do —
                              take my wife's boots, glassy
as a crow's eye, which I can't forget seeing
shuffling across the floor
of a cowgirl bar in Great Falls, Montana. Spanish boots, I remember,
with silver heels and toes,

Spanish boots, high-topped, waxed to a crow's eye.

                              ____

All morning the tiny petals of these pears
shake off in the wind, flicker and drift, as though their own small witness
is to shame us into faith...
                    In middle age, truly,
it's all a grueling miracle, the spirit sagging like a bag of cut grass,
or curling on itself like an old boot...

Everything struggling, yes,
toward severance, it's odd what the memory smuggles into the afterlife —
the squeak of my mother's hospital shoes,
or a baseball game from the fifties, my father's wing tips
kicking up a coaching box —
                    pocket charms against oblivion,

and I'd not want to forget these pear trees dusting the driveway,

the pickup, the yard,
                    or my daughter on her toes, rattling
light from low branches, I'd not forget
these petals like soggy pearls
                    clinging to her shoes.

———

When my wife was a child, she was ashamed of her shoes.

Southern California, mid-sixties…
                    so picture Easter with orange trees,
lemon, oleander, eucalyptus, picture small daisies
in bright window boxes along the edge
of the desert, red hue in the morning light, blue in the evening,
and now a second grader, a little girl with one dress
salvaged from a house fire
                    and worn all year to school.

Imagine shoes to match, and Easter in a child's mind.

Sure, some children have less, but put yourself in that child's mind
and picture the Cadillac pulling
into your graveled drive.
                    Surely you'd remember the crunch
of those tires, your Sunday-school teacher's teal and gold sandals
tracking the sandy grass,
and certainly for the rest of your life
the huge double doors of that Palm Springs mall revolving
into a city of light —
                    fountains of brass cherubs,
chandeliers, skylights, and that one fragile storefront of glass
where every wall sparkles with shoes.

O Mandolin, *O Magnum Mysterium*

Ah, the music of the spheres, the old Jew quipped, plowing his walker
down the pawnshop aisle.
                              Whatever, I nod,
and cradle the beautifully scarred mandolin in my open palms —
rutted ebony fingerboard, caramel-grained face of rusty spruce,
two strings missing, bridge cracked.
                                        Torture, I thought, teaching myself
to play this thing, then pondered all the other agonies
it must have endured —
the lovers wooed and lost, the bottles dodged
in barroom discourses,
                    loneliness of widowers on their porches at night,
their hard music rising in starlight.

String pluck and fret buzz — the sound of a spooked bird.

I turned to the window to read through dust its history in scars,
my face, no doubt, the mug of a doubter.
So what, pleads the pawnbroker,
                              you'll have the mystery.

                    ———

Or was that misery? The way the world guards its secrets, I mean, giving
grudgingly here, withholding there —
                              thus the mandolin,
disobedient, miscreant,
which might as well be the mystery of suffering itself.

So a little seclusion now, for thought, on the wooded bank of Triplett
      Pond.

High overcast shredding,
                    and a sudden freckling of sunlight
and out of the shallows under the rock dam a mallard taxis off the water,
climbs and banks,
                    gone over the high wall of hardwoods.
Stray crow far off, mockingbird closer…
and the mandolin trilling out the indecipherable harmony of things.

I glare at the dark-grained teardrop from the luthiers of Gibson —
too short for a boat paddle,
                    too heavy for Ping-Pong.
How charming, though, the polished and sunburst face,
the delicate snowflakes pearled
along its neck,
                    its melancholy little sparrow-cries
fluttering over the riffled water. O mandolin,
                              O Magnum Mysterium.

—

Years ago in Macon, Georgia, I lived below a guy who played the
      mandolin.

Old Victorian on Coleman Hill, run-down
and broken into apartments,
                    bad plumbing, suicidal staircase.
Late at night
          and early in the morning, as though they were expecting
a guest, the notes of his mandolin crept down the stairs
to linger on the landing.

Sometimes I'd open my door and let them in — tunes I'd never heard,
Mozart maybe, or Bach,
                    then something out of some Gypsy songbook.

Once, though, late, I marched up to bitch —

room darkened in candlelight,

                     stench of wine and stale cigars,
then peeking around the door, a bearded turnip — middle-aged, balding,
rimless bifocals balanced on his nose.

A flower, a bottle. A portable typewriter on a little pine table
candled like a shrine,
and edging that candlelight a room of ragged books — Swedenborg,
Dante, *The Tibetan Book of the Dead.*

Steppenwolf in Macon? Playing Mozart on the mandolin?

                     ———

Ah, the music of the spheres, the old Jew quipped,

                     or maybe *that* was misery.
And what a grim Jeremiah the memory turns out to be, dragging
its sack of ashes

             out toward the edges of eternity, spilling an irony here,
a tragedy there, when what we need most often
is a simple psalm.

Out of the woods behind my chair

                     a hiker drags onto the path, old guy
       sagging
in sweatshirt and gym shorts. He nods, huffing, gawking
at the mandolin, which chirps right on with
its garbled melody,

             picked up now by the mockingbird across the cove.

Down the path he waddles and vanishes into the trees.
Adiós, chimes the mandolin,

                 ciao, adieu.

                     ———

Every tune's a farewell, says my friend Steve Belew,
a lament, a dirge, a requiem...

Then what does the memory have up its sleeve?
What does it mean to do
                              with that man upstairs and his ladybug
         mandolin?
Those mournful baroque notes?

Or this picture I've kept of him alone,
near dusk,
              at a kitchen table wobbling on a short leg, his elbow tipping
a bottle to a glass
                  as he stutter-counts like a man
half-dopey for sleep the houseflies crawling his cabinets and dishes,
his crusted cans of sardines and chili,
                                    to discover, finally,
how this might go on forever, all time darkening
into a stained light
shattered by the window, unless...

                              ____

Clink and slow gurgle —
                      neck of bottle, lip of glass —
and the greasy walls tilting their greasy tulips this way and that as the
         chair
slides an inch, the table rocks,
and a misbehaving elbow
                      knocks the mandolin to the floor...

Listen. Creak of the chair
as the soul leans out toward the open window. How many times already
has it pitched its little tirade
of abandonment?

Little soul, says Epictetus, *bearing about a corpse.*

And how stubborn it seems now, and impersonal,
pigheaded, pitiless.
                Not the would-be corpse, no,
sodden with booze and slouching already on the windowsill,
but the cocked revolver rising in its palm.

———

Viper thoughts, viper thoughts, a phrase I caught from Coleridge...
unless there is only the world,
                        and after that, the absence of the world.
The mockingbird, and after that, the absence
of the mockingbird. The mandolin...

And this endless chirping
across the water — alarm of the spirit or simple praise?

———

Across the cove
                the baggy geezer in gym shorts stumbles out of the trees.
He parts the branches and sits
on the weedy bank. On the green water his reflection is lost
in the reflection of trees. Legs crossed,
he stares at a sunken limb struggling out of the water.

Wind riffles the water and doesn't disturb him. The jay in the thicket
doesn't disturb him,
                or the rowdy mandolin,
or the mockingbird, or the single crow high in sun-glare.

How still he sits, legs crossed, staring. Who knows what music
he's listening to now? Who knows
but he's succeeded finally in renouncing the world

and is listening this moment to Jesus
                                    or Buddha?

And who knows if he sees the low branch bobbing, the shadow pouring
itself into the water,
                    the moccasin, black as a tree root, glistening,
its beauty a witness to the world's sense of irony?

Along the jagged bank it plows a subtle
but quivering wake. Watch out, bullfrog. Watch out, philosopher.

Allatoona Storm

for Edward Hirsch

The sun had crossed the wide lake. Thunderstorms every afternoon
for a week, and now black clouds mobbing again over the distant marina
where one jinxed bass boat jerked at its rope.

In the book in my lap a pyramid was being stacked, stone by stone,
in a desert. Tons of limestone on sledges,
ramps, ropes, the grinding timbers,
                              unthinkable human misery...
I scratched my head at the lives wasted on immortality.

And in Egypt, it said, no historical evidence for the presence of the Jews.
No plagues then, no exodus, no forty years kicking around
in the wilderness —
                    so forget about the walls of the parted Red Sea
crushing Pharaoh's chariots, startling as it was in Technicolor.

Sure, they had the facts. It was history, archaeology.
And from there I might've quibbled with plenty of lovely pictures
in my illustrated Old Testament —
                              the ostrich following the elephant
into the clumsy ark, the bolting prophet in the belly of the fish —

but the sun over the lake was slicing through the clouds
in such a miraculously thin veil,
                              and the rose trellis lifted to the thunderbolts
the waxy faces of penitents, and all evening
the stooped magnolia, leaves gray as sackcloth, trembled...

Kenny Roebuck's Knuckle-Curve

Slow and goofy as the kid himself, it rises out of crowd-noise and memory,
wobbles off the mound in a long jerky float
                                    like the face of a drunk
coming out of a bar, luminous under streetlights,
rising, dipping, weaving,
                        hovering over sidewalk and oily street,
closer, closer, until gradually you see it's a face
you know, a face
you've mourned in the mirror —
                        stitched, battered, scarred —
the very mug of failure, but floating now in hard-won abandon,
lost to the world, recklessly at peace,
easy to swat as a saint,
                    and you rock back, swing,
and it hops, weaves, jerks,
rockets at your crotch, and once again the world isn't what you think,
and the memory, already wobbling, knuckles off
into voices, laughter, jeers,
                        that sobering pop of the catcher's mitt.

The Undertaker

Where could he go after the showroom emptied at Holcomb Chevrolet
and the doors on the service garage
                              clanged down for good?
Only the street of small shops and drugstores, only a gas station
or a grocery — or that one sprawling house
at the head of Main, where he'd learn to dress and powder the dead.

No one wanted this. Not my mother, not me.
We knew they'd follow him home, clinging like dust to his shadow.
They smelled like formaldehyde,
                              sardines, stale tobacco.
They left a film my mother couldn't sweep away.
It stuck to our shoes. Made us edgy, tearful.

—————

Sharp words flew, toast burned, the laundry scorched.

But slowly, as we grew used to the dread, the intensity
of the shadows flooding the house,
everything else intensified also —
                              his brutal hugs in the evening,
my mother's silence crackling into laughter,
the vivid sizzle of bacon on the stove, the purple violets
in our jelly glasses. It wasn't just spring, I know that,
or the freshly scrubbed windows, or the sunlight turning orange
through the rusted screens —
                              it was those guests
we couldn't coax home, forever darkening some corner,
sheepish, nervous,
                    desperate to be offered a chair.

In the Big House of the Allman Brothers
My Heart Gets Tuned

for Kirk & Kirsten West

Visitors sleeping in strange rooms
                                        may themselves be visited, surprised
by a gauzy and uninvited guest, a curious gray eye peering
over a dusty chiffonier.
                                Visitors sleeping, yes, or trying to sleep sometimes
may be startled, the muted walls, the closed
and padlocked closets, even the floorboards seeping
from their scars
                        something knowable only in the dream.

After twenty-eight years I find this out, buried in goose-down quilt
and memory in a bedroom of a house
I stood outside of once
                        to hear through bricked Tudor wall
and blanketed windows an electric concussion of bass
and guitar.
                Steam off the asphalt, I remember,
and that white blur of dogwoods along Vineville, sparkle of mushroom
in magnolia shadow,
                        bells of Saint James, blue jay chatter,
and me on the spidered sidewalk,
a kid, hero-struck...

                            ——

Struck, sure, and dumb,
an edgy tangle of high-voltage nerves, ragged-out in blue jeans
and frat jersey,
                bloody ankles, bloody hands,

16

wired and tripping, two-stepping backward in Mexican sandals, a
      long blaze
of hair off my shoulders, sombrero left hanging
on the MG gear knob.

But perhaps you, too, in some freaked-out greed for vision
or grace, have found yourself
                            chewing a mouthful of crabgrass, stupefied
and afraid, skulking on all fours those briary terraces
of Rose Hill Cemetery to pause on the edge
of a crumbling wall
                and see in blue half-moonlight
the granite slab of Elizabeth Reed tarnishing under the charcoal trees...

Held breath and audible heartbeat...
tree frog, night bird, tractor trailer groaning
                                    far up the interstate,
and at the foot of the hill, in that lush pit of shadow,
the river like a loose tongue.

                        ____

I'd stumbled down
those terraces to the bricked crypts bordering the railroad tracks
and river. *Little plazas cool as courtyards,*
Borges says,
            prowling through the mausoleums of Recoleta.
Rhetoric of shadow and marble, inviting enough, sure,
but at night in Rose Hill, in those alleys
of maimed angels, a shabby Victorian dignity bordered on indignation.

Still that music of river and something else...
that late bird, far off,
                    like a whistler lonely in the afterworld,
little prelude, little curtain-opener,
and I waited for an hour on a marble tomb,

                                        drooling weeds, watching
through a canopy of water oak
the half-moon ringing a light show over the far ridge of pines,
opening act for a no-show.

Looking for the dead? an angel drones,
Don't look here,
            nobody home.

                        ——

But these rooms famously spirit-filled —
                                    that anonymous woman
with her basket of wildflowers, climbing
and descending the stairs, the boy in torn knee breeches, the dead brothers
themselves caught more than once, rocking
against the staircase banister.

Grand and terrible, Jung hails
the hereafter —
                thus, *unperturbed by the grief of the bereaved,*
that *icy silence* of the dead.

Terrible, yes — witness brother Gregg, panicked and trembling,
as the eyes of Duane's photograph
trailed him down the hall,
                        the very way we tremble when we're ripped
from a nightmare and hang for a moment
between two worlds.

                        ——

Shadow-lace fluttering the ceiling, shifting star and circle,
diamond, oval, eye,
                and who wouldn't expect to see them again here
in their own house,

their features drawing shape from those shadows —
muttonchops and mustache
                              of Howard Duane Allman, deep gaze
I met one morning eye to bloodshot eye
in a Kmart on Riverside,
                              and those honey-sweet eyes of Berry Oakley,
sunken and calm as an effigy.

Such reticence, though, such pity in their silence,
neither touching the flattop
                              worked from its case and propped,
like a calling, against the wall.

No, neither touching a string, though something is playing the bones
of this house — strung-out memory
or middle-aged panic —
                              as I listen near the corner of sleep
to the heating pipes, to the creaking floor beams and roof beams shifting
toward the rhythm of my breath,
                              as though the house,
my heartbeat, the larger night, were all tuning up for the lifting
of some curtain,

the way one guitar will lean toward another
in those final, unnerving moments
of rehearsal...

Shooting Rats in the Afterlife

But to that other realm, writes Rilke,
alas, what can be taken?
                              A bitter hull I chew on frequently out here
under the Bradford pears, much to the bliss of the sweat bees
        and mosquitoes.
Nothing, the old poet swears, not a cracker, not a crumb,
but I don't know,
the memory is so persistent, and territorial. Take Macon, Georgia, 1971,
which I carry around in my head, like a classic video.

I remember the long scraped field waiting to be crossed,
the scattered garbage glassy in starlight —
old tires and oil drums, a bassinet, a toaster, a shadeless porcelain lamp —
and the red clay
                    that sagged like a spent mattress under our tires
and took on, in the starlight, the clotted glaze of blood.
At the far end of that field
huge hills of garbage waiting to be dozed, a little paradise of vermin.

                              ____

Nothing, not a cracker, not a crumb. Still
a vague intimation shadows the memory of this place, and others,
that somewhere down the pike these landscapes are waiting again,
or are, perhaps, the only things we take with us —
our psychic terrain —
as though through memory we create our own afterlives —
which can't be the entire breadth of it all,
                              but in some way a homeland,
a landscape out of which we might ramble into the afterlives, yes,
the memories, of one another...

———

Much to be said for the pleasures of the soapbox
and the splinters,
                    which cart back through the memory an apple crate
I preached from one morning.
Seven years old, in the yard behind the outhouse
behind my grandfather's store,
the locally popular fires of Gehenna spouting off my tongue.

I don't recall the congregation — a couple of guineas, a laying hen or two —
only the cadence of my trance,
                            and the slats of the apple crate
swaying up and down, threatening to crack...

Once I read about a saint who'd accomplished the similar — preaching
to the animals, I mean.
                    Though what he preached, I don't remember,
which isn't the real question anyway — rather why I've dawdled so long
on the highway to sainthood,
                    why the potholes and road signs
haven't shown more clearly in my headlights.

———

In those truck lights, only garbage — tires, oil drums, waterlogged books,
broken china, a stroller missing its wheels.

We cut those lights when we left the road. We crawled, windows down
in August heat.
                    Heavy stench like scorched butter. No breeze.
We rode slow,
though everything moves slowly in the memory.
Which is part of the act of savoring, the way you might turn
your ex-wife's engagement ring
slowly between your fingers

to let each facet spark fire.

Which is not to claim every memory a jewel, though it sparkles
like garbage in starlight,
only to say that we have it again,
                                        a moment given back
to turn in our heads, over and over, letting
each old detail catch new light.

———

Over and over those hills of garbage gleaming diamond, sapphire,
        emerald…
Small appliances
                shining like silver plate…

but what I'd like to get back is that sermon to the guineas, that fire
unleashed in words. Yes, the Word,
though I don't recall Christ teaching much about animals.
Still, calling his children *sheep*,
                        some animals he must have loved.

But rodents? Who knows?
And being a good Jew, he displayed no love for swine, demonizing
a whole herd and driving it over a cliff. But here accounts differ,
history fades, the complexities
of theology multiply —
                        approaching, no doubt, the number of angels
that could dance on the head of a rat.

All of which says little about the hierarchy of souls, or how memories
become jewels
                we cherish in eternity…

———

And nothing more about dominion over the animals,
or even good sportsmanship,

                    which, by the by, never crossed our sights.

How far we parked from those mounds of garbage
depended on the booze,
and here too the memory blurs — only barrel-glint of pistol and rifle,
and the quiet sag
of drunks leaning against bumpers,

                    all but one drunk, yes,
all but Leroy Lawson, home on furlough,
who stood at ease by the driver's door and leaned
into the rolled-down window.

Patience then, and the heavy breath of silence...
three minutes, five, until finally
that small scratching —

              softly at first, around the low edges, then louder
as it seeped toward the center and up
until every foot of garbage rattled with it, and Lieutenant Lawson, cocking
his Ruger, leaned into the cab

              and jerked on the headlights —

———

In Paradise, say the Southern Baptists, every crown is jeweled, every jewel
a good deed remembered,

              a kindness rewarded.

A sweet thought I've loved,
but anybody's guess. These jewels, though, stud my memory:

Leroy Lawson leaning into that truck, then salvo of headlights
blinding against garbage

              hundreds of startled rubies...

2

Homage to Buck Cline

At the edge of town,
past Landers' Rexall Drugstore, the road whipped right then hard
    downhill
over the tracks of the L&N Railroad,
                                and one night in '65,
stoned on a glass of Mateus rosé, with spaghetti
homemade by my girlfriend's mother,
                            I gunned it for the thrill of the dip,
and peeled a little rubber coming back to the road…

Up ahead the river, the Etowah,
                    and the buttery glaze the moon spread
across the concrete railing of the bridge,
then the traffic light at the corner of the North Canton Store,
where sour Buck Cline
                sat in his dark patrol car with the gold badge
of the Canton Police stenciled on his door,
                      waiting for some Romeo,
Don Juan, some small-town Lothario, to run the light
in his father's Impala…

Yes, so much relies on the imagination…

and what troubles he mulled
                those tedious midnights, wrangling in
the rowdies, the would-be toughs
circling the Burger Chief
            in their jacked-up street rods.

———

And imagination, of course, depends on so much…

Take the polished memory of my grandfather's horse barn
with its hayloft full of jewels,
                              or the pasture and the riding ring, the
        dog lots
full of beagles, the swaybacked chicken houses crawling
with mice,
              with cockroaches, slugs, with maggots of the dream-life…

Or Mr. Cantrell on the floor of his South Canton greenhouse,
his hands churning clods in the glazed filth.
I remember, yes,
              the good rose requires good filth.

So you'd drive by slowly under the green signal and give Buck a nod,
and maybe in the dark cab an eye would flare,
                              or not,
having come to what he'd come to in middle age, making
his poor living
              out-toughing the tough.

_____

Call it perverse, Poe would,
                    that heady surge of folly that clobbered me
at the light as my foot revved and lifted and the V-8 squalled
under the jumping hood.

What else to say about that rush
                        in my heart as I caught Buck Cline
looking up from his clipboard in the dark car backed into shadows…

then the light going green
                    and me pulling out, turning left,
and the long slope of highway past the Burger Chief stretching out
like a drag strip under the stars…

Perverse, truly.

Three miles from home and a quarter-mile lead, and I floored it, barking
off some Firestone for the Burger Chief crowd,

> forty-five, fifty-five,

and Buck growing smaller in my rearview,
eighty no sweat, and who-knows-what at the top of the hill,
nothing on me but darkness

> and the curve past the rock barn,

the straightaway sloping toward the South Canton bridge,

nothing but the darkness my headlights butchered,
then tiny in my mirror

> those blue lights throbbing…

———

Had the stars ever been so frazzled
and on fire, there on the shoulder of Highway 5 with our headlights killed
and the towered lights of the Pony League ballpark
long gone black,

> only two small taillights far behind and fading?

Crickets and a rush of wind

> and under the bridge, the river rounding

the big flat rock where Ace, the shoeblack at the Canton Barber Shop,
fished on Sundays in his ratty straw hat,
then the light in my face

> and the growl behind it…

Shut up, he'd ask the questions…

> And did,

glaring over the beam of his flashlight at the license I'd had for a month.

"You been drinking, boy? Didn't see me back there?"
"No, sir. No, sir," and over the trees
beyond the river,

the stars flared and calmed and flared again
as he glanced from the license to my face and back,
breathing my name twice, or my father's...

"Reckon your daddy'd like to get you out of jail?"
"No, sir." "No, sir" to everything,
and the dizzy stars
                    flaring again over the hazy trees,
the river jeering where the big flat rock jutted under the shadowy bridge
and deep under the current
                    the blue catfish wallowed the mud...

———

Something divine in the memory:

all those dusty little windows of the brain opening inward,
a mirror inside a mirror
                    inside a mirror. *Glimpse Into Eternity*, read the sign
at the Cherokee High School Science Fair,
and when you leaned into the peephole of the big black box
taller than your head,
                    somehow your eyes kept going and going...

———

Once in a theater line in Marietta, Georgia, an old saw from my hometown
shaved off some conversation.
                    Sunday evening, early nineties,
and across the square lush with dogwoods
the bells of the First Baptist chimed
                    an old hymn, far off, but loud enough
to bend him closer.

Something about his eyes I've remembered,
pale, but sharp,

the streetlight under the bleached stars catching them
in that gleam of deep reverie — like the eyes of a scientist,
or a saint,
                    when the clouds finally open...

"Your old man," he said, "you should've seen him play football,"
meaning Canton High, 1941,
                         the fall before the war.

Everything was in those eyes,
                              and that word he edged toward, the way
he uttered it with such reverence over the church bells,
as if he'd tasted its weight
on his tongue for years, careful for the perfect usage,
that true word that said it all — "Tough."

                    ____

And stayed tough enough
even after the war
                    when the shrapnel gnawed into the small of his back
with every step he took
up or down the service ramp at Holcomb Chevrolet, every step
he took across the concrete garage
on that splinter of a bone
                         the Japanese navy left in his leg,
that memory always alive and violent, though never spoken,
having in its pain too much of the divine,
                              the unapproachable...

                    ____

Tough also one night
at Little League when a drunk behind the backstop kept deviling the
        umpire —
big man in overalls, a mill worker, hard, poor, angry,

all the desperate adjectives,

          and the words frothing out merciless and ugly,
and the man's own boy at the plate
trying to see the baseball through that rain of curses,
until the umpire, Doyle Fowler, threw off his mask and charged around
the backstop,

        the man, though, the mouth, had picked up a shovel,
and caught him with the blade
square in the face,

        and my father, out of the dugout, fallen suddenly
on him, the mouth, the drunk,

          arms around him in a wrenching hug,
not out of anger, but something else,
and them on the ground,

        the one man weeping,
and my father talking, not shouting, but talking quietly
and hugging the whipped man harder and harder,
as though he'd known all along

          a secret the man thought no one knew...

———

Like the generations of leaves,
Homer says, *the lives of mortal men.* Or something close, and that night
whole generations trembled

          under the nervous stars as Buck Cline,
like a slightly stunted Ajax, leaned down
and speared me in the eyeball with the beam of his flashlight.
"You think you can whip my ass?"

I shook my head.

        He held out the license like a gift,
"You think you can whip your daddy's ass?"

I shook my head again,

        looking up where his pocked and shadowed face

blocked the glare of the moon.

———

Maybe in the long haul,
as a friend says, most everything blows off steadily to the shoulder
of the road and wallows like litter
                              in the dark we leave behind, things
that have disheartened, haunted, obsessed, delighted,
until finally there's nothing to distract us
from that last curve opening
                    onto the homestretch...

I agree. To the shoulder of the road, to the shoulder, but always waiting
to fly out of those gullies
                    on these sudden and unaccountable gusts...

———

And so much hangs on it,
                    the way memory toughens us up for that tumble
and drift of eternity, for the unpatrolled landscape
of the psyche unfurling,
                    and so much, certainly,
on those unknown connections, far back, we used to credit to the stars...

Buck Cline,
            how many charming stars in your crown?
One certainly for the night you spared me
for my father
            on the graveled shoulder of Georgia 5
with the bloody moon's own halo glowing around your head.

Saint Buck, I kept saying all the way home, and lit in an uncluttered niche
of my memory
            a little shrine... Saint Buck
of the handy blackjack,

Saint Buck of the billy, of the speed trap, of the dark patrol car lurking
in the shadows,
                    troubled patron of would-be toughs,
of war heroes and weeping boys,

street cop, surely, of the City to come...

3

Melville in the Bass Boat

...meditation and water are wedded for ever.

Three hours I drifted the black cove, throwing deep runners, live shiners,
rattle-bugs and jigs,
                    a Vienna sausage, a pickle,
a mustard-soaked sardine, and for all my stealth and trickery,
failed to conjure
one small mystery caged in the bones of a fish.

                              Never mind,
there was a book in the bottom of the boat, a paperback, slightly soggy,
and I propped the rod and primed the lantern.
                              Over the oily lake
the stars burned only a little dimmer, though soon
I glowed in a buoy of light.

Wind off the open water, and wave-slap. Boat-drift then
and the tiny *Pequod*, fat-sailed,
                    "plunged like fate into the lone Atlantic."

                    ———

Sizzle of crickets, cicadas harping from the far pines,
and occasionally out of that directionless dark,

                              one curious owl quizzing
those nameless voices of the cove.

Over the blending rhythms of water and word,
over "that deep, blue, bottomless soul,"
                              how easily the mind drifts...

Then spark and slap of the dream-fish, leaping far out, like a thought,
and the felt vibration in the nerve,

                      that trembling to know, to take
another crack at whatever might surface — that mind-flash,
that "ungraspable phantom of life,"

                  that bony metaphor.

Little Drop of Wickedness

Ruckus around the bird feeder — two greedy mockingbirds mugging a
        cardinal —
and a small wind whirling
                up from the creek beyond the cul-de-sac,
but no other disturbance, no ado,
no alarm but my heart going off at the presence of my guest.

This morning, yes, a visitor under my pear tree and cherries,

when I walked out to read my novel under my canopy of blossoms and
        leaves,
a visitor beside my table, a stranger,
                   unexpected, unnerving, coiled
like a wreath on a root-knee.

I edged under the canopy
and sidled toward my chair, and his spoon-head bobbed into my shadow.

Odd to say how benevolent he looked and languid
with his fat jaw
            draped over the hourglass ridge of his back,
and how gently he offered his gaze,
                how congenial his greeting,
as though all my fears were fallacy,
and the history of evil,
        some pathetic bamboozle.

———

Ah, how wily the serpent's smile! quipped my grandpa
as he raised his double-barrel to the pine branch
                and blasted the coachwhip
onto the roof of our chicken house.

He found a dead branch and raked the snake down.

Muscled and thicker than a boy's fist,
                                        shiny black
as if coated in motor oil, it gleamed as he turned it in the sun.
Not poisonous, he said, but a snake —
                                        the serpent, the deceiver—
and certainly the eater of chicken eggs.

He held it up, let me look, then flung it into a briar patch.

Under my canopy of blossoms a guest had made himself comfortable.

A lord of the underworld,
                        says Lawrence of the creature drinking
at his water trough. Here though, to be more precise,
Agkistrodon contortrix, which,
granted, could be the name of some minor Greek god.

Leaf-stir and quivering light —

and his head turns slowly as I slide toward the chair
where he studies me, sizes me,
                        ponders with his small tongue my human
        folly,
deciding, perhaps, whether to share
with a stranger
                the drop of wisdom ruminating in his jaw...

Have you heard above the wind
the sound of the Lord God
                        walking in the garden in the cool of the day?

Have you heard a distant rumble and a sigh like rain in the trees?

In the war, says my pal Steve Belew,
you could hear that rumble for miles rolling through the jungle...

─────

My wife's paralegal, a lonely woman and middle-aged, chats up guys
in the cyberlounges
                        and met one in New York for a weekend rendezvous,
some honcho boss for a labor union in Houston.

Chinatown and Little Italy,
and the night lights over Broadway fractured by a thin mist of sleet...

Then a restaurant, she says, like you see in the movies
and dancing in a bar of dim blue light,
where they tendered each other,
                          as Ring Lardner crafts it,
a smile with a future in it.

─────

Agkistrodon contortrix, copperhead,
                         lover of brush piles and fallen logs,
stone heaps, old tires, flat rocks beside cool water,

lover of field mice and fat lizards,
frogs, gophers, skinks, lover of my naked heel in nightmares of fishing...

His split tongue tastes my blood in the air. His spade-head finds
a shaft of wormy light,
                    the psychedelic blossoms shiver.

I ease between the arms of my chair. If I leaned down only slightly,
I could touch the tip of his tongue.

─────

Not a big snake, no, not a honcho, not a boss,
but a snake —
                    the serpent, the deceiver—
whose split tongue seems to know me, whose slit eyes seem to know…

His head bobs right,
                    then back, as it follows the toe of my boot.
He will not take his eyes off my boot.

———

The next evening they walked along Central Park
while the full moon chaperoned
over the high-rent skyline, and later window-shopping, came on a coat,
a man's coat,
                    full-length suede with a fox collar.

He stood on the sidewalk and gazed at the coat.

He gazed at her
                    and she could tell it was love. And what a picture
he made turning like a gangster in the full-length mirror,
the very man the coat was made for.
                                        But the price, well…

Then the charge card hovering above her purse,
and she sees it and wants to put it back, the coat is too expensive,
has she lost her mind…

Already, though, it's found the salesclerk's hand.

———

Satan is real, croons Ira Louvin, on a '58 recording for Capitol.

Yes, and kicking still in '69 when my pal Belew,
drunk and sore-hearted,

ran across him peddling smack in a Saigon bar.

Clearly Middle Eastern, says he,
                    and at a distance
well-groomed, red blazer quite snazzy against his salt-and-pepper beard.
But under the bar lights
                    the jacket goes drab, soiled, thin in the elbows.

Still, how benevolent he looks through that cloud of yellow smoke,
his loose jowls
                    sagging under his stringy beard,
how congenial his smile, how gently
he offers his gaze...

Fame or riches? the usual proposition.
                              But Belew, the skeptic,
only knocks back his brandy, *So where does evil come from?*

Depends entirely on your point of view.

                    ——

Yes, but an old horse
I would've whipped a little harder, whipped with a knobby stick.

So easy to misread the world's mixed messages —
these blossoms going electric in the shivering light, the red tongue
        bobbing
on the scaly stem...

That's right, paleface, world speak with forked tongue,
and the serpent, swears my grandpa,
will always strike.
                    True, the way a man might spit on a woman
in an airport terminal, and tell her she's fat and ugly
and disgusting to see naked on his bed,

43

and that he's keeping

                the coat because it looks so good on him
and seems little enough compensation
for a weekend spent

                slobbering on a sweaty slug.

——

A drop of the world's poison, wisdom from the serpent's jaw.
True, but only a drop.

                Wicked and bitter, but a drop.

I edge my boot toward the rusty nose,
and *Agkistrodon contortrix, lord of the underworld*, rears into a shadow,
shifts and rears again,

                reading the air with his tongue...

A drop of the world's poison,

                    hovering, swinging, waiting to fall,
as the little spade-head, the fanged rusty teaspoon, rocks back
and forth with the toe
of my boot, gauging my threat,

                bluffing some bravado.

Then wind in our canopy —

                blossom and quivering light, hiss
and mouth-flower blooming, so easily misread...

Disobedience

No, not that door — never!

Ice on the door latch, and ice in the splintered grain of the pine.
Which is to say winter has hung on now well into March,
which is to say, Montana
                          and the wind slapping drifts over the sheep pasture,
the crisp stars frenzied with grief on the tar-papered sky.

A noise now from the barn, a hoof against a stall —
the old ram with the broken horn. He smells trouble again, a thief
on the snow,
              the stench before the stench of blood.

The owl we used to keep time by is far off now, timeless.

No, we can't stand here on the stoop too long,
not even in a dream, or a memory.

                          ——

Ice on the latch.
Then the rasp of the pine door, swollen, swinging on its crippled hinge.

Go on, you've come this far, though nothing's changed —
quarter-moon scar on the floorboards
                          where the door needs planing,
the Chinese rifle, handy for coyotes, hung by its sling on the coatrack,
one lamp, as always, warming the great room.

And he's there again by the window, at the wagon wheel turned into a table,
leaning over his stack of wooden matches, spirit re-fleshed
and calloused,
              clipping the blue tips

into the matchbox, wiping his knife on a flannel sleeve.

Wind jabs the door, scattering sawdust and dirty snow.
He doesn't look up.
He lays out the matches, one by one — a ramp, a wall, a roof for the depot.
A matchstick ladder leans

against a soup-can water tower.
Don't expect him to look up.
Don't expect a nod, a smile, a tip of the grim railroad cap
tilted low over his glasses.

Only close the door behind you now. Stand
and watch. For as long as you can stand to watch.

And said once himself, looking over a book of photographs,
What's a memory but a taunt?

————

Wait, he's moving his hand...

over a mountain and a waterfall frozen
against the face of a mountain, and in the valley
all those little buildings of Ohio matchsticks — red with gray roofs, green
with red roofs —

sprawled across the snowy table.

Soon now the mail train can tunnel its way through the mountains,
and the postmaster sort packages

for the hardware store and the pharmacy.
Here in the village of no misunderstandings, a man pauses
on the sidewalk and knows where he stands.

A picket fence now for the preacher's house, a street sign, a parking meter,
then a door for the diner

where the eggs are always over easy.
The smells of three bakeries drift up and down the blocks.

Listen —
in the church below the mountain, the rattle of voices
thawing into parts around tambourines,

                                    guitars, a wood-burning stove —
the prayer chain rattling for a deacon's gout, a drunk,
a disobedient daughter.

                    ———

Then the letter again,
on the end table, under the lamp, half-buried in a wallow of fliers and
        bills —
the gray envelope,
                    your best stationery, hand-marbled,
from that little shop off the Piazza San Marco.

Yes, that's your loopy cursive
and the wildlife stamp commemorating the glory of the wood duck.

Don't go through this again, please.
                              No more
of the eternal *if only*...

                    ———

Memory a taunt?
A hard moment, yes, but a hard man, a hard father? I don't know...

But out the window, look,
out by the used-lumber dump where the windmill's shadow needles the
        snow,
the old truck again,
                    long past revival, rusty as a sheep turd.

Remember the sticker on that bumper?

Wipe away the snow —

If it ain't the King James, it ain't the Bible!

———

And if it ain't the Bible? Well…

So even if the envelope had been opened, and the gray feathery letter
unfolded under a lamp,

even if the heart had struggled
an extra hour in the light, even if the ram
had chased away the shadow crossing the snow, and the ambulance driver
finished leisurely in the cafeteria

his grilled cheese and coffee…

No, really, no more of this eternal *if only.*

———

The world, sighs Mr. Warren, *is the world it is,*
and the memory, therefore,
must be the world *it* is. And the dream, yes, the world *it* is…

and so in this memory of a dream
the old man can never glance toward the kitchen and the creaking door
or feel across his cheek

the cold slap of remorse,
but must always glare silently over a town and a valley of his own dream
to a ranch between two mountains,
where an old ram, in a tin barn,

bleats at some thief in the snow
and the shadow of a windmill sweeps a sturdy log house
where the prosperous father
of an obedient daughter

tilts back in his sheepskin recliner
and counts, like sheep, his blessings.

Andalusia Visit

for Bill Sessions

Look out! my nightmare shouted,
as she crashed across the porch, flailing the shadows with a crutch.
Dark wind blew a storm of dust, or feathers, and lightning
through the rusted screen
                              flared off the lenses of her glasses. *You're not Billy,*
she said, jerking around twice,
                              rolling her neck like a peacock...

But the room had collected,
and that first filmy light through the curtains of the French doors offered
        only
my familiar brass and tarnished footboard, the spool-backed rocker,
the sunburst afghan
                    my dog had chewed into a rag...
No, wherever the dream had swept me,
                              someone else had been expected...

and I remembered she'd written:
I went to Communion for your intentions on Friday the 8th
and have been praying for you since.
                    Coming into the Church
must have its terrors...

Terrors? Yes, and oddly that lightened my own.

Somehow in the dream I had stumbled
                              into another man's afternoon,
another man's storm, but had come back startled and blessed,
the way someone leaving confession might slip

into the wrong raincoat
                              and find himself walking an unfamiliar street,
the clouds departed, the stars
above the brownstones more passionate than neon,
his head clearing,
                    his deep pockets bulging with possibility.

Black Hawk Rag

All morning by the kitchen window
prowling the neck of the mandolin for the misplaced notes of a tune —
big wind after cold rain
                       and half the leaves on the sugar maple have
     tumbled
onto the wet grass. The mandolin whines like it wants to fly south.

Twice this morning I almost had the bridge —

so the old garage beside my grandfather's store, streaks of dusty sunlight
through warped clapboards, smell of stain
and sanded wood,
               fiddle notes like warblers in the rafters —

then blue jays deviling some squirrel at the feeder, or the garbageman
scraping the can on the curb.

Silly to lean on the rhythms of memory,
which will hardly give back
                    even the threads of that rag. But what else
to suggest he's still in that garage, hunched
in a shadow, fiddle
under chin, waiting for my ghost to swing through the door?

Vigilance

for Barry Hannah

All morning in the secret place
among the jays and finches biding their time at the feeders,
the cardinals, the towhees,
                        the stray mosquito and the sweat bee,
the pacified Lab with her beef joint
and the long caravan of ants
                         trekking the wilderness of needles and dry grass.

First scent of the Bradford pears and the pink dogwoods opening,
the cherries, the magnolia, all the old magicians
honing their tricks,
                     as the leaves cloud and clear my pages
like the shadows of passing saints…

Days now I've pondered
what my mother-in-law calls the Endtime, and the limp millennium,
which has simply rolled over
                      like a grizzled dog in front of a fire,

days now trying to make the Jesus of Mark
jibe with the Gospel of John…

——————

Meteors last night.

Rocked back in a beach chair in the front yard, I watched them
scratch across the black sky.
                     Down the street
the rough grate of skateboards and Rollerblades, the smell of meat grilling

over charcoal. A brassy music, something Latin,
drifting off someone's deck...

So what was that twinge in the chest? Hope, distress?
All this searching for the Kingdom of God...

Out there or in here
is what I need to know, whether those capacious taunting celestials
are only pointless sizzles, or if one, maybe,
inconspicuous, faint as a pinhead,

               is a blue Parousia unfolding.

         ———

A neighbor of mine has a sticker on the bumper of his pickup —
If there hadn't been a Pearl Harbor,

             there wouldn't have been a Hiroshima,

which, he swears, has something to do with the signs, with hymn
and holy trumpet sweeping across the cosmos.
Perhaps, though, somewhere
               in the dark matter of history, a synapse
or two has shorted out. Spark and sizzle,
spark and sizzle...

How to stitch together those loose connections?
So much stress on the needle-bone of faith...

He's a quiet man, my neighbor, who fights in his garden
a low-tech battle with ruin,
            hand hoe, spade, garbage bag...

         ———

I'm fairly low-tech also, believing
that the old truths are never old-fashioned,
               believing they just show up

each season in a fresh cut, a new fabric — sandals and robe
or flip-flops and jersey.

I watch and wait,
follow the common recipe for vigilance. Yes, *if the goodman of the house
had known in what watch the thief would come...*

—

One night in a cancer ward
in Oxford, Mississippi,
                    Jesus appeared to my friend Barry Hannah.
I've neglected you, Barry said, and Jesus,
a tall man, barrel-chested, nodded quietly, or simply stared —
I've forgotten the whole story.

He told me this on a patio in Sewanee, Tennessee,
and because of his face
I wasn't surprised to hear it spoken so casually between a swig from a shake
and the lighting of a cigarette,
                    because of his face, I think,
still glassy from the chemo, like the face
of a man come home from a war, not tired exactly,
                                        or anything
I'd call fearful, more the face of a man who's discovered in his scars
something terrible, or something holy.

—

Which put me in mind of my father-in-law
on his paper route
                    in northwest Montana. Icy night and stars like silver neon,
mountains dropping to valley and the occasional paper tube
leaning out of the emptiness...
                    Suddenly in the headlights of his truck
Jesus standing on the shoulder of the road.

He came home weeping.
He staggered out of the kitchen, spilling his coffee, struggling
to describe those strange eyes, that glazed face,

                               not tired exactly, or afraid,
but more like someone stunned, or hurt,
the face of a man
            who's seen in his wounds something terrible...

—————

These are the blessed, yes, the fortunate witnesses, the ever-abiding,
who have found in their rucksacks

                          enough to tide them over,
while I too often perch
among the scribes and Pharisees, flustered with argument,

or rail like Flannery's poor Misfit, frayed
and wrathful, drawing down
on the grandmother
            his beautifully empirical resurrection theology —

It ain't right I wasn't there... if I had of been there
I would of known...

—————

And though I scratch my head profoundly,
                         I cherish also the smaller
    witnesses
and hold under my cap the conjectures of Mr. Emerson
who divines among the daily
a necessity in spirit
           to manifest itself in material forms...

Thus once or twice a year we see Him in the clouds.
A picture crops up off UPI, a storm churning the edge of a California
    desert.

And, yes, if you turn it just so

a face comes out in the wallow

of shadow and light. Or someone in Chicago or Philly

has caught again in the evening glare off a high-rise

a suspiciously holy profile.

Yes, accolades also to the minor mystics

who spiritualize the world's minutiae.

Like my neighbor again who grew a yellow rose

wilted with the sign of the cross, or his sister in Biloxi

who once saw the Virgin swimming

in a bowl of vegetable soup.

Accolades, yes, to Ramona Barreras

of Phoenix, Arizona, who pulled from her oven in 1977

a tortilla scorched with the face of Christ,

which may or may not

have been the face that appeared

some ten years later in Bras d'Or

on an outside wall of a Tim Hortons restaurant,

though both made the papers

and drew their share of pilgrims.

———

Spouts portly Mr. Blake, *every thing that lives is Holy!*

Which any backsliding Hindu could tell you...

But what does it mean that God keeps stamping his image on pastry
and French toast,

on biscuits lightly burned around the edges?

———

Once my mother-in-law dreamed

she was floating down a river on an outhouse. True. The water rushing in through a half-moon window,

                                              wild buck and kick of the current,

then somewhere up ahead, in fog
and darkness, the prodigious rush of a waterfall...

It was not the Jordan, she says, but claims it still as a sign.
Who knows?

I listen in the dream and in the world. I watch
and wait, turning over rose petals,

                                       scrutinizing taco shells, piecrusts,

these constantly mutating faces in the clouds
gathering now

                   in their own dark way over the suburb.

———

Wind-gust and a sprinkle of rain, and such a strong scent of pear tree
and cherry whipping across the yard,

                                  it feels like the world

has re-upped on its lease.

Such a drawn-out and low-key unraveling of the sorrows —
small earthquakes in California, a mudslide in Mexico,
famine, yes, but always famine,

                         and the hundreds of little wars flagging up

and firing out...

And these centuries of slowly accruing misery?
Vigilance, I say. Vigilance and virtue, or what we can muster —
and the moon will not give its light, and the stars
will fall from the sky.

Yes, says the old woman, stirring her cocoa,
If the owner of the outhouse

                         had known when the river would flood...

Three-quarter Moon and Moment of Grace

Family asleep, I walk my worries into the shallow yard.

Coal smudge of bird feeder and barbecue, bony oak and maple cluster
in their velvet funeral clothes,
and through their arms
                            the moon throwing down its pearly river…

Yes, that pocked eye watches everything drift away —

the child dreaming of new shoes, the cop rocked back in the cab
of his cruiser, and you also,
                            in your chair by the shaded window,
even these heavy-freighted houses cruising low through the suburbs
where a middle-aged man, playing mandolin,
limps barefoot through his yard,
                            baffled and grateful.

———

Waltzing through the Endtime, my mother-in-law calls it,
wringing out my spirit
                    like a dirty dishrag…

Yes, I've always fretted the small stuff,
and of the thirty thousand souls that depart the earth daily, only three
enter Paradise — or so teaches Jesus
in The Gospel of Bartholomew.
                            A bleak assessment, true,
not even the odds you get in Vegas, so I remind myself constantly
who failed to make the final four.
                            Canonical selection, I mean.

And for a plan, a road map, a strategy, who wouldn't prefer John —
Jesus come back to share with his friends

                              a breakfast of fish, a little chat,
then ciao again,
off to ready a suite in the Waldorf Hereafter?

Verily, verily,
doesn't it all come down to memory... Bartholomew's
or John's, yours or mine? And what are we dragging in that heavy sack
if not the cornerstones of Heaven,

                             or the charcoals of Hell?

———

Tree frog and cicada, and far off in the brushy shadows of the suburb
the deep clarinet of the mourning dove...

                          Wind and leaf-shiver,
then all noise loosens into silence.

Listen, out of the crank and rut
of history, this opulent millennial stillness —

                          as though the Great Mind
after long concern lingered on the edge of a thought,
which in its complexity
may seem to us only more drifting, everything washing away
in a current of light...

                        these thin and final sparrow-notes of the night
tumbling like leaves over patio and shrubbery,
your hand rising with mine

                    on the same gust of wind...

ABOUT THE AUTHOR

David Bottoms was born in Canton, Georgia, in 1949.
His first book, *Shooting Rats at the Bibb County Dump*, was
selected by Robert Penn Warren as winner of the Walt
Whitman Award of the Academy of American Poets. He is
the author of six other books of poetry and two novels.
Among his many other awards are the Levinson and the
Frederick Bock Prizes of *Poetry*, an Ingram Merrill Award,
an Award in Literature from the American Academy and
Institute of Arts and Letters, and fellowships from the
National Endowment for the Arts and the John Simon
Guggenheim Memorial Foundation. He lives with his wife
and daughter in Atlanta, where he holds the Amos
Distinguished Chair in English Letters at Georgia State
University. He is Poet Laureate of Georgia.

The Chinese character for poetry is made up of two parts: "word" and "temple." It also serves as pressmark for Copper Canyon Press.

Founded in 1972, Copper Canyon Press remains dedicated to publishing poetry exclusively, from Nobel laureates to new and emerging authors. The Press thrives with the generous patronage of readers, writers, booksellers, librarians, teachers, students, and funders — everyone who shares the conviction that poetry invigorates the language and sharpens our appreciation of the world.

Major funding has been provided by:
The Allen Foundation for The Arts
Lannan Foundation
National Endowment for the Arts
The Starbucks Foundation
Washington State Arts Commission

STARBUCKS
FOUNDATION

THE ALLEN FOUNDATION *for* THE ARTS

NATIONAL
ENDOWMENT
FOR THE ARTS

For information and catalogs:
COPPER CANYON PRESS
Post Office Box 271
Port Townsend, Washington 98368
360/385-4925
www.coppercanyonpress.org

CPSIA information can be obtained at www.ICGtesting.com
Printed in the USA
LVOW11s2104310715

448373LV00004B/15/P